SOUTHERN MAIN LINE CAMERAMAN

(*Frontispiece*) One of the author's favourite pictures — a powerful study of rebuilt 'Merchant' Navy No. 35009 *Shaw Savill* at Exmouth Junction Shed waiting to work the 'up' 'Atlantic Coast Express'.

SOUTHERN MAIN LINE CAMERAMAN

W. PHILIP CONOLLY

Edited by Mike Esau

Oxford Publishing Co.

(*Title Page*) Although the 'Lord Nelson' class was not common on the Waterloo to Exeter line, particularly west of Salisbury, Eastleigh Shed did have a duty which included a stopping Salisbury to Waterloo train. Here No. 30861 *Lord Anson* passes Tunnel Junction, Salisbury on such a working. The line to Southampton diverges to the left, and the 'T' sign marks the end of the speed restriction on the approach to the junction.

ISBN 0-86093-365-2

Typesetting by:
Colin Powell Typesetting & Design, Bournemouth,
Dorset.

Printed in Great Britain by:
Biddles Ltd., Guildford, Surrey.

Published by:
Oxford Publishing Co.
Link House
West Street
POOLE, Dorset

No. 30907 *Dulwich* was one of the St. Leonards' 'Schools' class
transferred to Nine Elms in 1957 following the completion of the Hastings
line dieselisation programme. No. 30907 coasts downhill towards
Salisbury with a stopping train from Waterloo.

(*Right*) The author's brother watches T9 No. 307 leave Woking with the
3.54 p.m. train from Waterloo to Basingstoke in about 1946. The volume
of parcels and packages on the platform underlines the importance of the
railway as a general carrier after the war. In later years, when it was often
formed of only three coaches, this train was worked by the King 'Arthur'
class, and towards the end of steam on the Southern, Bulleid Pacifics.

FOREWORD

Following the success of Philip Conolly's first book of pictures, 'London Midland Main Line Cameraman', which was published by Allen & Unwin in 1982, I have assembled a selection of his best Southern work. Sadly Mr Conolly is not in the best of health at the present time, and has asked me to write a few lines to introduce his photographs.

Philip Conolly grew up in Southern Railway territory at Battersea, although his interest in railways, and particularly his special affection for the LMS, and subsequently the London Midland Region, was fired by childhood visits with his father to Euston. His father bought him his first camera in the 1920s, and so began many years of fulfilling railway photography.

His primary interest has always been in main line trains, which in the days when there was so much to choose to photograph, had the action and glamour which most branch lines lacked. Those readers who have seen his London Midland book will know how well Mr Conolly's photographs not only capture the atmosphere of time and place, but also show railway staff at work, an aspect which most railway photographers neglected. The photographs in this book are equally broad in their scope, and cover a period of some thirty years up to the mid-1960s, but with the emphasis on the fifteen years or so after the war, a time when the enthusiast could enjoy the widest variety of locomotives and services. The reader should be able to find around fifty different types of locomotive in this book.

Limited time for his hobby meant that it was not possible to visit all lines, so the majority of the pictures in this book are taken on the Western Section of the Southern. Mr Conolly was particularly fond of the Salisbury to Exeter line, a route full of interest with its branch connections, and along which locomotives made exhilarating downward dashes before the next climb to Hewish or Honiton. What a superb line this would be for 1980s' main line steam, and it takes little imagination to picture No. 35028 *Clan Line* at grips with Honiton Bank again!

It was on this line that his favourite locomotives worked, the 'Merchant Navy' class in their rebuilt condition, and several feature in this book particularly some on that most romantic of trains, the 'Atlantic Coast Express', or the 'ACE' as everyone knew it. All Mr Conolly's visits were made by train and then on foot, using the valued lineside photographic passes which the Southern issued in the days of steam. Without independent transport, the range and scope for a railway photographic trip was limited in those days, and it is interesting to reflect how relatively remote and difficult of access were lines like the Salisbury to Exeter, even in the 1950s. Nowadays a car, and the motorway network, enables the enthusiast to photograph trains hundreds of miles apart in a single day, or follow a main line steam special over the entire length of its journey. But after arriving at some wayside station behind steam, there was nothing to equal a day of leisurely lineside photography, and to enjoy in a quiet way, the countryside and the passing trains.

I grew up on Southern territory at Malden and spent many exciting hours on the bridge to the east of the station filling in my *Ian Allan ABC*. Selecting and printing the pictures for this book has therefore given me particular pleasure and revived half-forgotten memories. Although we did not know one another till long after, Philip Conolly and I sometimes used the same train to go up to Waterloo in the late 1950s, the 6.37 a.m. from Basingstoke which stopped at Malden at 7.52 a.m., invariably hauled by a work-stained Urie H15. This train provided what must have been one of the shortest main line steam runs in the Southern suburban area, and travel on it in a comfortable Maunsell or Bulleid coach made a fine start to the day.

Unfortunately, Mr Conolly has lost all the original details on his photographs, so it has not been possible to date the majority of them. The absence of information has made caption writing a little difficult, and responsibility for any errors which may have slipped through the net is mine alone. Finally I would like to thank Derek Winkworth for his generous help in providing information during the course of my research for the captions.

Mike Esau
March 1986

It is with much regret that I have to report that Philip Conolly passed away on 1st August 1986 after a long illness. I hope that this book, and his earlier *London Midland Main Line Cameraman*, will be a lasting reminder of his talent as a railway photographer.

Mike Esau
August 1986

TAKING
WATER

Watching locomotives taking water was always enjoyable, especially when the hose was thrown down from the tender, and the water remaining in it gushed out. The fireman of 'Schools' No. 30923 *Bradfield* carries out this manoeuvre at Basingstoke Shed after filling the tender.

'West Country' Pacific No. 34031 *Torrington* takes water at Salisbury whilst the driver oils round, and coal is shovelled forward ready for the journey west. The engine has a 5,250 gallon tender which it received when rebuilt in November 1958.

Most of the M7 locomotives in the 30667 to 30676 series spent their final years in the West Country. No. 30669 is taking water at Tipton St. John's on a train from Sidmouth, whilst No. 30674 is on station pilot duties at Salisbury. No two water columns ever seemed to be built to the same pattern, as the pictures on these pages show.

READY,
STEADY,
GO!

Some half-way between Waterloo and Exeter, Salisbury was the natural change-over point for locomotives and their crews. The very dusty coal on the tender of a 'West Country' Pacific is shovelled forward ready for the run to Waterloo. The lower picture shows the high eves of the unmodified tender which tended to obstruct clear passage of the water column hose on to the tender. From the footbridge, an interesting view was possible of the top of No. 34008 *Padstow*, showing the safety-valves and the position of the whistle. In typical style, the locomotive then slips violently on oily rails as the regulator is opened despite the use of its sanders.

WATERLOO

(*Right*) 'Battle of Britain' Pacific No. 34059 *Sir Archibald Sinclair* is ready to leave with the 1 p.m. West of England express, composed of green-painted BR Mk. 1 stock. No. 34059 was withdrawn in May 1966 after a varied career, being on loan to the Eastern Region in 1951 in its unrebuilt form. The engine went to Barry in October 1966, but left for the Bluebell Railway thirteen years later, where it is being restored.

(*Below Right*) Standard Class 5 No. 73116 *Iseult*, named in 1962, leaves with the 12.54 p.m. (SX) train to Basingstoke, a train that might have been worked by its 'King Arthur' namesake No. 30749 a few years earlier.

(*Above & Below*) The author often used this train to start a day of photography along the line. 'King Arthur' No. 30779 *Sir Colgrevance* is waiting to leave Waterloo on the 7.20 a.m. train to Salisbury, where it arrived at 9.58 a.m. The coaching stock is typical for a train of this type – one Bulleid set and possibly a van at the end.

VINTAGE SOUTHERN

The two portions of the 3 p.m. train to the West of England at Waterloo in the late 1930s, headed by 'King Arthur' No. 455 *Sir Launcelot*, and 'Remembrance' No. 2330 *Cudworth* provides an interesting comparison between the front ends, the N15 looking altogether more substantial.

(*Above Right*) The small 5ft. 7in. driving wheels of K10 No. 391 show up well in the picture of the locomotive in between duties on the Windsor side lines at Waterloo in the 1930s. One of a class of 40, No. 391 was built in July 1902 and lasted into BR ownership. The locomotive is fitted with a Drummond 4,000 gallon bogie tender, although the majority of the class had the smaller 6-wheel variety.

(*Below Right*) Headed by 'King Arthur' No. 780 *Sir Persant*, a West of England train waits to leave from the 860ft. long Platform 11 at Waterloo. Together with Platform 14, which was the same length, this was the longest platform at Waterloo at the time. The old 'A' box spans the lines in the background and another 4-6-0 locomotive can be seen waiting to run back to Nine Elms Shed.

LONDON TERMINI

(*Below*) Attractive patterns of water on the platform set off this picture of 'Schools' No. 30938 *St Olave's* at Charing Cross with a short Sunday morning train to Hastings. The train will make a slow exit from London, stopping at Waterloo and London Bridge, before running fast to Tunbridge Wells (Central).

(*Left*) Within whistle sound of Trafalgar Square, Bricklayers Arms' 'Schools' No. 30926 *Repton* is pictured at Charing Cross with the 8.25 a.m. train to Hastings in the early 1950s. The night has been foggy judging by the lamp at the end of the platform.

H class, No. 1263 is pictured at Victoria one sunny morning with the stock of a Newhaven boat train. No. 31263 finished its days at Three Bridges Shed, working trains on the line to East Grinstead, and is now preserved on the Bluebell Railway. At the other end of the train, 'Schools' No. 30929 *Malvern* fills the station with smoke as it prepares to leave.

DIESELS

No. 15232 was one of a 1949 English Electric/Bulleid diesel shunting design for the Southern Region, and is seen shunting at Bevois Park, Southampton, set off by a fine array of LSWR signals controlling the yard. Sister engine No. 15244 may be seen on the Lavender Line at Isfield in East Sussex where it is being restored.

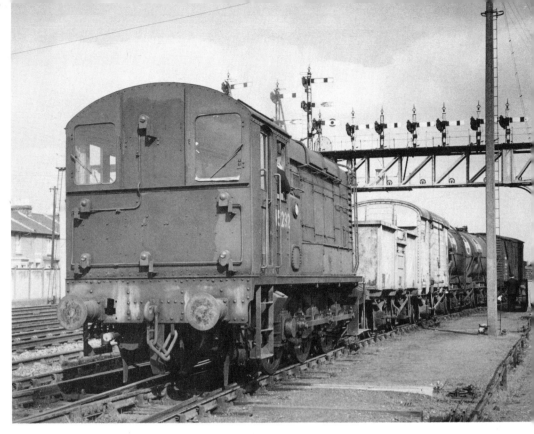

In the spring of 1953, LMS diesels Nos. 10000 and 10001 were sent to Nine Elms and worked in conjunction with Nos. 10201-3, mainly on West of England line trains. No. 10000 is on such a duty at Salisbury waiting to leave for Exeter. The faces of the spotters seem to register suspicion about this new arrival.

No. 10201 arrives at Exeter (Central) with a 'down' train. All five diesels had been transferred to the London Midland Region by 1955.

Raworth/Bulleid electric locomotive No. 20003, introduced in 1948, presents a picture of cleanliness on the Newhaven boat train at Victoria. The driver is cleaning a front window prior to departure, and the two fold-down headcode discs indicate Victoria and Newhaven Harbour.

THE 1948 LOCOMOTIVE EXCHANGES

Together with No. 35019, No. 35017 *Belgian Marine* worked some trains on the King's Cross to Leeds route in May. Here No. 35017 is seen on the approach to King's Cross, near Wood Green, with the 7.50 a.m. train from Leeds, composed of fifteen coaches. The locomotive is fitted with an LMS-pattern tender containing water pick-up apparatus.

Class A4 Pacific No. 22 *Mallard* is pictured on the 10.50 a.m. Waterloo to Exeter train near Raynes Park on the 8th June. This locomotive was replaced by No. 60033 *Seagull* after failing with a hot inside big end at Salisbury the following day on the 'up' return working.

Rebuilt 'Royal Scot' No. 46154 *The Hussar*, fitted with an Austerity type tender, is seen passing the Southern Railway sports ground at Raynes Park on a trial run with the same train as No. 22, in June.

Ex-LMS 'Duchess' No. 46236 *City of Bradford* passes Surbiton with the 'up' test train, the 12.37 p.m. 'Atlantic Coast Express' from Exeter on either 23rd or 25th June. Plans to transfer the engines to the Bournemouth line in the 1960s came to nothing, to the disappointment of enthusiasts.

THE 1953 BULLEID PACIFIC FAILURES

(*Left*) During the temporary withdrawal of the Bulleid Pacifics in 1953, due to the failure of an axle on No. 35020, the Southern Region borrowed some LMR Class 5s, ER V2s, and WR 'Britannia' Pacifics. Cardiff Canton's No. 70029 *Shooting Star*, temporarily based at Exmouth Junction, leaves Salisbury with an 'up' special, whilst V2 No. 60917 arrives with a 'down' special. By way of contrast Drummond T9 No. 30288 from Eastleigh Shed waits to leave with a Southampton line train.

(*Above & Below*) A Crewe North Class 5, No. 45350 prepares to leave Yeovil Junction with the 3 p.m. stopping train to Salisbury. At Salisbury, Class 5 No. 45216 from Bank Hall Shed arrives with an 'up' local train. The use of this class on the line anticipated the arrival of the Standard Class 5s a little later. The full list of LMS Class 5s allocated to the Southern Region was Nos. 45051/61, 45130, 45216/22/3 and 45350.

'FOREIGN' MOTIVE POWER

Towards the end of steam on the Southern Region, LMR locomotives were dealt with at Eastleigh Works. Ivatt 2-6-0 No. 43088, seen here on the 'down' main line at Micheldever, was recorded as being in the Works in May 1965, and may be en route for attention.

On 4th September 1964, 'Jubilee' No. 45595 *Southern Rhodesia*, worked a Preston to Weymouth pigeon special, here seen entering Southampton Central Station.

Fairburn 2-6-4T No. 42100 is seen at Clapham Junction with the 7.14 a.m. Tunbridge Wells West to Victoria train, composed of Maunsell stock and a SECR 'Birdcage' set. These locomotives replaced elderly Brighton designs on these trains, such as the I3, J1 and J2 classes. A 4-SUB electric multiple unit, No. S4626, is in the opposite platform with a Shepperton to Waterloo train.

A 9F No. 92205 was one of three of the class allocated to Eastleigh in December 1960 to work Fawley to Bromford Bridge tanker trains. In this picture the locomotive is being used on a Feltham to Salisbury freight, which includes a diesel shunter behind the engine. Like so many of its class, No. 92205 had a short life, being built at Swindon in May 1959 and withdrawn in June 1967.

In perfect weather on 15th September 1963, a memorable special train ran from Victoria to Horsted Keynes hauled by Caledonian Railway Single No. 123 and T9 4-4-0 No. 120. Here the pair are beautifully captured getting into their stride through Clapham Junction. The whitewashed coal on the Single can clearly be seen. Photographers on the platform out of sight to the right of the picture were thwarted by the passing electric train, and thus missed a 'master shot', as it would be known in modern parlance. The two locomotives are now at opposite ends of the country. No. 123 as a static exhibit in the Glasgow Museum of Transport, where it has been since 1966, and No. 120 is in a new guise as No. 30120, and is currently at work on the Mid-Hants Railway where it is a great draw for enthusiasts.

CITY M7s

(*Left*) The Nine Elms M7 locomotives quietly carried on with the unglamourous duties around Waterloo and Clapham Junction for many years, and were only missed by enthusiasts when more modern motive power took their place such as Western Region pannier tanks and BR 82XXX 2-6-2Ts. An M7, No. 30132 passes the now demolished flats at Vauxhall with an empty stock working for Clapham Junction, formed unusually of WR and LMR stock, whilst No. 30241 is on a 'down' vans train.

(*Above & Below*) Nos. 30241 and 30039 (carrying a 71A Eastleigh shed plate) are waiting their next turns of duty at Clapham Junction and Queens Road respectively. Both engines were built at Nine Elms, No. 30039 in May 1898 and No. 30241 in May 1899. The side view of No. 30241 shows the comparatively large size of this engine, a fraction over 35ft. in length.

CLAPHAM JUNCTION SOUTH WESTERN SIDE

Nine Elms duty No. 68, carried by H15 No. 30489, included the 7.40 a.m. empty stock and vans train from Clapham Junction to Southampton (New Docks) which is setting out on its journey on a cold winter morning having just gained the main line.

The 'down' main line platform provided the best view of the ever changing scene, such as LBSCR E1 0-6-0 No. 2138, looking very work-weary, as it pauses between shunting coaches in the yard. No. 2138, originally named *Macon*, was built at Brighton in 1878, so would have had some seventy years service to its credit when this picture was taken in about 1947. Two lady cleaners appear to be enjoying a chat in the coach behind!

Contrasts at Clapham Junction over the decades, with West Country No. 34091 *Weymouth* passing on an 'up' boat train in the early 1960s, and T14 Paddlebox No. 443, in the carriage sidings some thirty years before. All but one of the T14s survived World War II, and No. 443 ended its days like the remaining nine members of the class, working semi-fast passenger and freight traffic on the main line out of Waterloo.

CLAPHAM JUNCTION BRIGHTON SIDE

(Right) On the same platform as the 7F, a C class, No. 31102, waits for the road. At the other end of the station J2 No. 32326 pulls away with a crowded early morning train for Victoria. Because the J1 and J2 classes comprised one engine each, there was always something rather special about seeing them at the Junction. No. 32326 was similar to No. 32325 but was fitted with Walschaerts valve gear.

(*Above & Below*) Although there was not so much steam as on the South Western side of the station, interesting locomotives could be seen. For example J1 4-6-2T No. 32325 arrives with a morning business train from Tunbridge Wells — note the trolleybus wires on St. Johns Hill. On the West London line platform, an LMS Fowler 7F 0-8-0 attempts the difficult start up the 1 in 166 gradient to Wandsworth Common with a freight to Norwood Junction.

THE SUBURBS

Almost at the end of the speed restrictions covering the approach to London, 'Merchant Navy' No. 21C15 *Rotterdam Lloyd* accelerates towards Malden with a West of England train, in 1946. The track on the 'down' slow line looks in need of attention, which is no doubt the reason for the speed restriction sign which can be seen in the distance.

A fine pre-war shot of 'King Arthur' No. 742 *Camelot* overtaking a 'down' electric train near Earlsfield. Some exciting pictures like this one could be taken given a little luck, and the choice of the right electric train departure from Waterloo.

Rebuilt 'Merchant Navy' No. 35005 *Canadian Pacific*, passes a 4-COR unit at Raynes Park, with the 'down' 'Bournemouth Belle'.

At Raynes Park more open vistas began to give way to the suburbs. Here 'Lord Nelson' No. 30860 *Lord Hawke* trundles an 'up' boat train composed of BR Mk. I stock towards Waterloo. The small board on the platform advises passengers for a 4-SUB electric multiple unit, 'Short train wait here'.

Two everyday scenes at Malden. One morning in 1953 M7 No. 30241 runs light engine from Waterloo to Esher to work the 10.10 a.m. 'up' empty stock. On the 'down' lines gangers carry out their inspection. The bridge in the background is unchanged to this day, and provides a splendid view of trains on this busy line.

The 6.37 a.m. Basingstoke to Waterloo train, referred to in the *Foreword*, was usually hauled by a Nine Elms Urie H15 class locomotive. It is pictured passing Wimbledon and starting from Malden after its scheduled stop. Due at Waterloo at 8.08 a.m., there was unfortunately no similar return working in the evening!

N15s
AT WORK

Before the arrival of the Standard Class 5s, 'King Arthurs' worked the majority of the stopping trains on the main line out of Waterloo. No. 30779 *Sir Colgrevance* leaves Fleet with the 8.21 a.m. departure — all stations to Salisbury.

No. 30773 *Sir Lavaine* is getting into his stride as the suburbs are left behind, to make an attractive picture passing Malden on a West of England train one winter's morning.

No. 30785 *Sir Mador de la Porte* has just stopped at Surbiton on a summer's evening with an 'up' train, whilst below, No. 30777 *Sir Lamiel,* runs through with the 7.14 a.m. (SO) empty stock train from Walton Sidings to Waterloo. Although the gradient out of the station towards Waterloo was only 1 in 378, the start could prove tricky, especially for the 'Lord Nelson' which stopped here at 8.04 p.m. with a train from Bournemouth.

WHEELS AND NAMES

Something of the solidity of construction of the 'King Arthur' class comes over in this picture of No. 30765 *Sir Gareth* at Basingstoke.

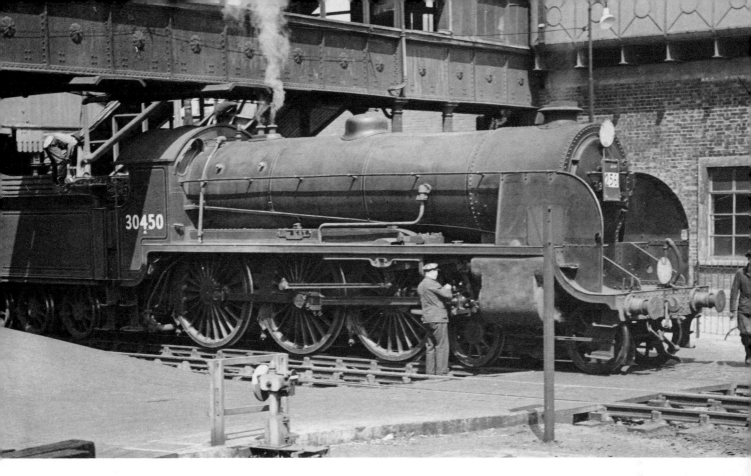

The driver of 'King Arthur' No. 30450 *Sir Kay* walks round the engine prior to departure from Salisbury, whilst below is a close-up of the middle driving wheel of this locomotive, showing the simple dignity of its nameplate. By 1959, the sight of a 'King Arthur' on a West of England express was rare. *Sir Kay* was withdrawn in August 1960 and was cut up at Eastleigh in October.

BASINGSTOKE

Basingstoke was a fascinating location on a summer Saturday with through trains to and from the Western Region. 'Battle of Britain' Pacific No. 34057 *Biggin Hill* pulls out past the shed with the 10.35 a.m. (SO) train from Waterloo, where a Western Region 'Hall' class locomotive is being prepared to take over a train on the line north to Oxford.

In the shed 'Schools' No. 30908 *Westminster* stands by the coaling tower after working a special train in 1960. This locomotive was withdrawn in September 1961 and cut up at Eastleigh.

'West Country' No. 34043 *Combe Martin*, fitted with a tablet catcher for use on the Somerset & Dorset line, appears to be on a train for the Oxford line, although the headcode is incorrect. The train is on the north, Great Western side of the station.

Once a common sight, a workaday S15, No. 30827 rumbles through the station with a freight for Feltham.

BOURNEMOUTH AND OXFORD

'Merchant Navy' No. 35030 *Elder Dempster Lines* runs into Bournemouth Central and past the shed with a smart train of Bulleid stock.

'King Arthur' No. 30740 *Merlin*, fitted with electric lighting, shunts a local train composed of LSWR stock. Judging by the time on the clock in the background, this could be the 1.10 p.m. (SO) all stations departure to Weymouth.

As now, many trains for the Oxford line and the north, via Basingstoke, originated at Bournemouth, especially after the closure of the Somerset & Dorset line. On a southbound working at Oxford, a Western Region 'Castle' has just retired from a through train in favour of the substantial presence of 'Lord Nelson' No. 30862 *Lord Collingwood*, whilst a neatly attired gentleman observes the scene from the 'down' platform.

Pressed into service on a summer holiday weekend, H15 No. 30491, rebuilt in 1927 with an N15 boiler, leaves Basingstoke with a through train for the north.

THE 'STRONG COUNTRY'

'West Country' No. 34097 *Holsworthy* passes through Micheldever on a bright summer morning with a Bournemouth train. The station is set in rural surroundings in the midst of the Hampshire chalk downland. The line to the station yard goes off to the right of the picture.

How many of you remember these famous signs like this one near Micheldever. The rebuilt Bulleid 'West Country' Pacific seems to have a questionable wheel arrangement! In 1963 the 'West Country' replaced a blue 'Merchant Navy' which itself took the place of a 'King Arthur' about 1951.

At Micheldever carriage shed, an ex-LTE Underground unit, bound for the Isle of Wight, peers gingerly at the outside world.

No. 35028 *Clan Line* climbs the 1 in 252 gradient through Micheldever Station with a typical Bournemouth line train of the early 1960s, one wet day.

EASTLEIGH AND SOUTHAMPTON

A line-up in the carriage sidings. Class 02 locomotive No. 30199, 'West Country' No. 34104 *Bere Alston*, the last to be rebuilt, and 'King Arthur' No. 30770 *Sir Prainius*, also notable as being the last 'King Arthur' to remain in service, make up the trio.

'Schools' class locomotive No. 30905 *Tonbridge*, fitted with a high-sided tender in 1958, pulls out of the station with a southbound inter-regional train.

An M7, No. 30053, is now in the USA, but before leaving these shores was stored outside Eastleigh Works in 1965 where this picture was taken. U class No. 31806, photographed at the shed, went for scrap to Barry in June 1964, but has survived, and enjoys an active life on the Mid-Hants Railway.

'Lord Nelson' No. 30864 *Sir Martin Frobisher*, blows off steam as it coasts past Southampton Airport ready for a stop at Eastleigh, with a semi-fast train for Waterloo.

A Q1, No. 33012, passes Eastleigh West box with an 'up' banana train from Southampton Docks to Nine Elms. Although adequately powerful for the job, the Q1 class were not commonly seen on these longer distance freight workings. More usually a S15 or H15 4-6-0 was employed.

In 1959, the Civil Engineer agreed to H16s using the Fawley line, and Nos. 30516 and 30517 were transferred to Eastleigh Shed in early 1960. No. 30516 is captured here passing Southampton (Central) with a freight for the line.

Round at the Terminus Station, Standard 2-6-4T No. 80087 shunts some vans.

ISLE OF WIGHT JOURNEY

Ryde Pier, pictured on a tranquil summer evening, as many like to remember it. The pier tram is racing the O2 locomotive on a train for Ventnor whilst, in the distance, a paddle-steamer has arrived from Portsmouth. The tide is well out, allowing the setting sun to cast a fine shadow of the train on the sand.

At peak times on summer Saturdays in the early 1950s, five trains an hour left the pier, two running through to Ventnor, the first fast to Sandown. At the end of the line at Ventnor, No. 28 *Ashey* is seen taking water under the shadow of St. Boniface Down.

Of such are the memories of childhood made — two young holidaymakers inspect the cab of No. 36 *Freshwater* at Ventnor, and below, the signalman has the token ready for the fireman of a Ryde train which is about to enter the 1,312 yds. long Ventnor Tunnel. In the tradition of country stations, the staff have been busy with the cultivation of hydrangeas.

BOURNEMOUTH TO WEYMOUTH

Wareham was the station for the Swanage branch. Q class locomotive No. 30541, now preserved on the Bluebell Railway, is seen pulling away with an eastbound freight. Below, M7 No. 30328 takes water in the 'down' main line platform before making another trip over the eleven miles to Swanage. The train is composed of an LSWR compartment coach and a Maunsell push and pull set.

(*Above Right*) 'West Country' Pacific No. 34040 *Crewkerne* pulls away from Poole for the last section of its journey to Weymouth.

(*Right*) Standard Class 4 No. 76061 pauses at Wareham with a stopping train to Weymouth. In the 'down' bay an M7 with a push and pull train provides the connection to Swanage. No. 76061, which was built at Doncaster, did not last until the end of steam on the Southern, being withdrawn in December 1966.

SWANAGE BRANCH

This Dorset country branch was rich in attractions as the following pages show — delightful scenery, an intermediate station, through as well as local trains, and a stone-built terminus and shed at Swanage, where the sun always seemed to shine during summer holidays. All success to the Swanage Railway of the 1980s.

A modeller's delight — exterior and interior views of Worgret Junction box where the branch diverged from the main line. Note the highly-polished condition of the metalwork, and a tin of 'Duraglit' is to hand!

(*Right*) An M7, No. 30328, approaches the box with a train from Swanage, and below, the signalman prepares to hand over the token to the driver of a Swanage-bound train propelled by an M7 tank.

An M7, No. 30111, i signalled for the 'up' ba platform as it approache Wareham with a train fror Swanage.

Another M7 pulls away fror Corfe Castle and through the narrow defile that markec the way to Wareham. The difference between the fenced off railway land anc the open heath is marked.

The fireman of M7 No. 30057 puts the injector on as the engine blows off impatiently one sunny morning at Swanage.

The crew of Q class No. 30541 will be able to enjoy the timeless view of picturesque Corfe Castle as the engine waits quietly in the station to cross a train from Wareham.

The minor road bridge to the north of Swanage Station gave a wonderful view of the charming stone-built shed and its turntable, where M7 No. 30107 is resting between duties during a hot summer's afternoon.

(*Above Right*) An animated holiday scene at Swanage Station with a through train for Waterloo at the main platform. To the left is a local train with an M7 0-4-4T, and strengthened by a Bulleid coach from which passengers seem to have just alighted for a day on the beach.

(*Below Right*) The driver of M7 No. 30057 attends to his engine after arrival at Swanage.

THE LAST 'LORD NELSON'

'Lord Nelson' No. 30861 *Lord Anson* was the last of the class in service, being withdrawn in October 1962, and cut up in November. On 2nd September 1962, the Southern Counties Touring Society ran a special train from Waterloo to Exeter where the class was rarely seen. In these pictures the train is seen at Salisbury on the outward leg of its journey. In contrast to the frantic behaviour surrounding special trains of the 1980s, the occasion looks a pleasantly relaxed one, with comparatively few people at the platform end, and by no means everybody is carrying a camera.

FIRST, LAST AND SAVED

No. 34110 *66 Squadron*, pictured arriving at Exeter Central from Exeter St David's, went into traffic in January 1951, and was distinguished by having the shortest life of all the Bulleid Pacifics, being withdrawn in November 1963. The first Pacific, 'Merchant Navy' No. 35001 *Channel Packet*, on the other hand, fared rather better, although it only ran for five years in its rebuilt state. The locomotive is seen passing Clapham Junction with a 'down' West of England train.

Luckier were Nos. 34051 *Winston Churchill*, saved for the National Collection, and 34067 *Tangmere* which went to Barry in March 1965 but was rescued in 1981, and is undergoing restoration on the Mid-Hants Railway. No. 34051 is seen on a 'down' goods just west of Wilton, and No. 34067 is pictured swinging round the curve at Battledown flyover with an 'up' train from the west. The additional plaque fitted under the cab number of No. 34067 is clearly visible.

ANDOVER CONNECTION

In the early 1950s, there were three through trains on weekdays over the 69 miles between Andover and Cheltenham, the old M&SWJ line. The U class Moguls were typical motive power for this line in its closing years, and No. 31794 is seen pausing at Swindon Town.

Some trains on the line were hauled by Western Region pannier tanks such as No. 8783 on a train from Andover Junction to Swindon, passing Red Post Junction box, built during World War II, where the double track M&SWJ line left the Southern.

An S15, No. 30834, pulls slowly out of Andover Junction with an 'up' freight for Basingstoke.

On the main line No. 34052 *Lord Dowding* passes Red Post Junction box at the beginning of the climb to Grately, with a train for Salisbury.

THE MAUNSELL H15s

In the heart of the Wessex chalk country. No. 30523 plods past Allington with an 'up' freight, whilst below, the same engine is seen at Andover Junction with an 'up' stopping train. No. 30523 was cut up at Eastleigh in February 1962. Although not quite as successful as the S15 class, these rugged engines were versatile, and could be seen on a variety of duties from summer holiday expresses to unfitted freight trains.

No. 30522 passes Brookwood with an 'up' freight train, a typical working for this class, which they performed competently and without fuss for many years.

No. 30524 runs light engine into Clapham Junction Yard before working the 7.40a.m. vans train to Southampton.

THE VERSATILE S15s

A fine picture of Feltham's No. 30510 passing Salisbury Tunnel Junction box one bright morning, with a freight at the beginning of the climb towards Grately.

(*Above Right*) Urie S15 No. 30512 is pictured near Fleet with the 9.45a.m. goods train from Feltham to Eastleigh.

(*Below Right*) On a wet Saturday morning, No. 30499 snakes out of Walton Sidings and on to the 'up' main line with empty stock for Waterloo, which will form a summer holiday extra. No. 30499, which was built in May 1920, ran until January 1964. After a period in Barry scrapyard it left in November 1963 for the Mid-Hants Railway. During World War II, No. 499 was one of three Urie S15s sent on loan to the GWR.

Redhill's No. 30835 coasts down Gomshall Bank with an eastbound permanent way train. The engine is fitted with a 6-wheel 4,000 gallon tender.

The Maunsell S15s were particularly suited to the Salisbury to Exeter line, and here No. 30829, always a Salisbury engine, is on a typical duty working a westbound freight at Buckhorn Weston Tunnel.

None of the 'down' side station buildings remain at Seaton Junction which is now closed, but the far concrete footbridge survives as part of a public footpath. In better days No. 30823 pulls out with an 'up' stopping train.

The slope of the North Downs forms a background to No. 30834 coasting into Gomshall and Shere Station with a train from Redhill to Reading. Since No. 30834 is a Feltham engine, and Duty No. 122, a Feltham duty, the engine probably worked eastbound from Reading or Guildford earlier in the day.

A T9, No. 30301, is pictured at the west end of the tunnel with a train from Bournemouth West. The tunnel, which is 443 yds. long, is situated between Tunnel Junction and Salisbury Station.

FISHERTON TUNNEL

At the opposite end, U class locomotive No. 31791 swings away from the main line at Tunnel Junction with a train for the Southampton line. No. 31791 was originally built by the SR as a K class 2-6-4T, No. 791 *River Adur*, but converted to a 2-6-0 following the Sevenoaks accident in 1927.

At Salisbury Tunnel Junction, Eastleigh M7 No. 30033 makes haste for the country on an unknown errand.

The lighting on 'Battle of Britain' Pacific No. 34052 *Lord Dowding* sets off its handsome lines as it passes Tunnel Junction box with the 3.15 p.m. Salisbury to Waterloo train.

T9s at WORK

During their last years, the T9s were regularly employed on the Redhill to Reading line. Here No. 30307 curves away from Shalford towards the main Portsmouth line with a train from Redhill, and sister engine No. 30310 coasts into Gomshall and Shere with a Redhill train, both composed of an SECR 'Birdcage' set, which was typical of the coaching stock in the early 1950s. No. 307 was lent to the LMS for a short period in 1941, probably to work on the S&D section.

At Salisbury, Nos. 30285 and 30288, both fitted with watercart tenders, are employed on trains to Bournemouth West. No. 30288, withdrawn in December 1960, was a candidate for restoration, but No. 30120 took its place. In the upper picture, Salisbury Shed's U class No. 31636 displays early British Railways livery.

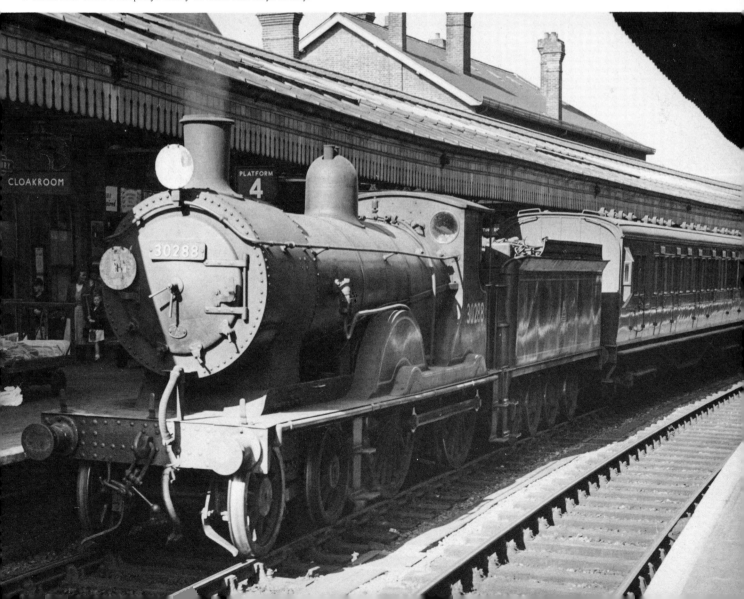

SALISBURY – ARRIVALS AND DEPARTURES

Western Region locomotives added to the interest of the workings to be seen at Salisbury, such as 'County' class No. 1000 *County of Middlesex* from Bristol (Bath Road) Shed, which is seen leaving with a stopping train for Westbury.

No. 34068 *Kenley* has steam to spare as it passes the 'C' box to arrive at the station with a short stopping train from Exeter.

(*Right*) At the other end of the station, 'West Country' No. 34034 *Honiton* is prepared for the run to Waterloo. Two men are shovelling coal forward, whilst two others top up the tender with water. No. 34049 *Anti-Aircraft Command*, in the next road, is fitted with a modified top smoke cowling.

'72B'

With the graceful 404ft. spire of Salisbury Cathedral in the background, the tallest in England, No. 35006 *Peninsular & Oriental S.N.Co.* passes the shed with the 1p.m. train from Waterloo to Exeter. With No. 35028 *Clan Line*, No. 35006 was the last 'Merchant Navy' to be rebuilt in October 1959, and survives to the present day at Toddington, in Gloucestershire.

(*Right*) Everyday scenes at the shed. Whilst S15 No. 30824 and 'King Arthur' No. 30774 *Sir Geheris* look identical from the front, the difference between the modified top cowling of No. 34049 *Anti-Aircraft Command* and the conventional No. 34038 *Lynton* is clear. Over fifty engines were shedded at 72B in the mid-1950s, including some eleven S15s, and the same number of Bulleid Pacifics.

BULLEID PACIFICS AT SALISBURY

The fireman of Salisbury Shed's blue-liveried No. 35009 *Shaw Savill*, which is preparing to take over a Waterloo train, exchanges greetings with the crew of No. 34055 *Fighter Pilot* arriving with the through train from Brighton. This arrived at Salisbury at 1.58p.m. in the early 1950s, so probably No. 35009 is going to take the 2.13p.m. 'up' 'ACE' departure.

(*Above Right*) No. 34049 *Anti-Aircraft Command* pulls away from the station with a train for the Portsmouth line, composed of LMR stock.

(*Below Right*) No. 35014 *Nederland Line* is passing the shed with what is probably the 9a.m. train from Waterloo. No. 34006 *Bude* waits in the shed for its next turn of duty.

'ACE' AND 'DEVON BELLE'

Having just passed the summit of the long 10 mile climb out of Salisbury, No. 35013 *Blue Funnel* comes through Grately with the (SO) Ilfracombe section of the 'up' 'ACE'.

Some six miles to the west at Porton, No. 35014 *Nederland Line* passes the station with the 'down' 'ACE'. The timings for the nearest 1985 equivalent to this train are only slightly faster. For example on M-F in the summer of 1961, the train left Waterloo at 11a.m. on a non-stop schedule to Salisbury to arrive at 12.23p.m. Today, the 11.10a.m. Class 50 hauled Waterloo to Exeter train arrives at 12.34p.m., but has made three stops en route at Woking, Basingstoke and Andover.

Engineering work was in progress at Malden when this picture of the 'Devon Belle' was taken, and the train is on the 'down' slow line. The elegantly-dressed lady in the observation car seems more interested in her paper than the passing scene and the prospect of lunch!

Shortly after its introduction in June 1947, the 'Devon Belle' passes Raynes Park behind a 'Merchant Navy' Pacific. Despite the attraction of Pullman car travel to West Country holiday destinations, its passenger figures were never quite up to expectations, and it last ran in 1954.

SALISBURY TO EXETER

Working an 'up' train, a neglected No. 34023 *Blackmoor Vale* speeds down the gradient through Sutton Bingham Station with steam shut off, possibly in preparation for a stop at Yeovil Junction some two miles on.

No. 34059 *Sir Archibald Sinclair*, emerges from the 742yds. long Buckhorn Weston Tunnel with a 'down' train.

No. 34033 *Chard* pauses at Wilton en route from Exeter to Salisbury, a journey which an all stations train typically took over three hours to complete. No. 34033 was never fitted with a coat of arms shield under the nameplate.

Standard Class 5 No. 73113 *Lyonnesse* coasts down the 1 in 80/250 gradient through Crewkerne with a train for Salisbury and Waterloo. The change in gradient from 1 in 80 to 1 in 250 through the station can clearly be seen in the train on the far side of the bridge.

WEST COUNTRY SIGNAL BOXES

Some 1½ miles west of Whimple, No. 35009 *Shaw Savill* working an 'up' express, passes Crannaford Gates box, which took its name from an adjacent farm.

Hewish Gates box was situated between Chard Junction and Crewkerne near the top of a long climb from Axminster, where the gradient eased from 1 in 120 to 1 in 160. The signalman is opening the gates for the passage of train.

Modernisation in progress at Exmouth Junction, with old and new signal boxes, and 1899-built M7 No. 30024 on an Exmouth train composed of BR-built suburban stock. The M7s were replaced by the new 82XXX class 2-6-2Ts in mid-1961.

A larger box was Exeter Central A at the east end of the station. No. 35016 *Elders Fyffes* is seen waiting to leave with an 'up' train. Perhaps because in those days railway photographers were comparatively rare, the signalmen seem to be more interested in Mr Conolly than the train.

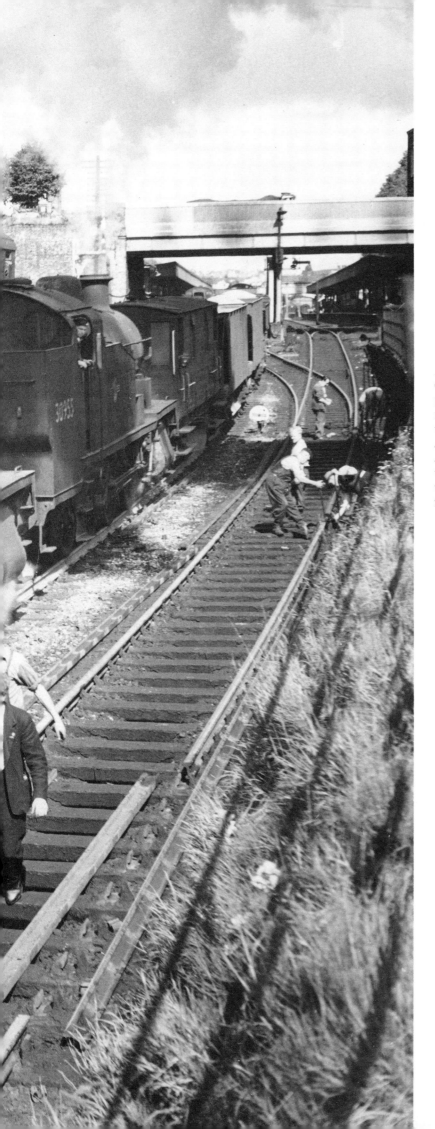

A bit of a panic is in progress outside Exeter Central Station. A rail has broken and the permanent way gang are working hard to replace it before serious delays occur to 'down' trains. On the 'up' line two Z class 0-8-0s bank a ballast train from Meldon up the 1 in 37 gradient from Exeter St. David's. The Z class took over banking duties in August 1959 until they were withdrawn at the end of 1962 in favour of the W class 2-6-4Ts.

ALL IN A DAY'S WORK

In classic pose the guard of a suburban electric multiple unit waves away his train at Malden. The sight of a guard deftly hopping on to his footboard as the train pulled out was always impressive. The picture pre-dates the painting of yellow warning panels on the front of these sets.

As recently as the late 1950s, water was still being delivered by train on the Redhill to Guildford line. At Ranmore Common, just west of Dorking Town Station, the guard of a Guildford train delivers full containers and collects the empties at a crossing keeper's cottage.

Among the varied duties of station staff would be the release of pigeons as here at Brockenhurst.

The guard of a train from Weymouth to Bournemouth makes a phone call at Dorchester South. This picture shows the site of the shed, and the separate location of the 'down' platform. The train from Weymouth in the picture is waiting to reverse into the 'up' platform which was built facing west when there were plans to extend the line towards Exeter.

SIGNAL BOXES

Two 'skyscraper' boxes. Sidmouth Junction with No. 34072 *257 Squadron* on an 'up' train. The Sidmouth line bay is to the left of the picture. No. 34046 *Braunton* is passing Tunnel Junction box on its cramped site at Southampton where the line from the Terminus station came in.

Of more substantial proportions was Wareham box, controlling the busy A351 road to Swanage. Frequent passage of trains on holiday summer Saturdays could cause huge traffic jams to develop. Here Standard Class 4 No. 76007 pulls out with an 'up' train.

On a fine summer's day, 'King Arthur' No. 30779 *Sir Colgrevance* is seen arriving at Oakley Station with its neat LSWR signal box, in charge of a stopping train from Salisbury.

SIGNALS

Attractive LSWR lower quadrant signals set off S15 No. 30844, seen coasting down the 1 in 80 gradient into Seaton Junction with an 'up' freight train.

Standard Class 4 No. 75078 and Class 3 2-6-2T No. 82019, both built for the Southern Region at Swindon, are captured in between duties either side of the SR pattern signal gantry at Eastleigh.

A Z class locomotive, No. 30951 shunts in the yard at Exmouth Junction. The left-hand side signal on the gantry controls access from the 'up' main line to the yard.

Still painted in blue livery, No. 35003 *Royal Mail* passes under a gantry of LSWR pneumatic signals at Fleet with the 'up' 'ACE'. These signals enhanced many a photograph along the line between Basingstoke and Woking.

YEOVIL JUNCTION AND TOWN

Although transferred to Nine Elms in 1959 as a result of completion of Phase I of the Kent Coast electrification scheme, 'Schools' No. 30913 *Christ's Hospital* is still carrying its 74B Ramsgate shed plate at Yeovil Junction whilst being prepared for its run back to Salisbury on a stopping train.

U class 2-6-0 No. 31637 is pictured outside Yeovil Town Shed. This class was ideally suited to the local passenger and freight workings from this depot.

For many years a Yeovil Town engine, M7 No. 30129 waits to leave the station with an auto train working to the junction. The M7s were replaced by WR auto-fitted pannier tanks in March 1963. In the shed yard U class locomotive No. 31805 rests between duties — note the neat wall of coal to the right of the picture.

Through services from the various branches between Salisbury and Exeter were long a special feature of this line. Here, 02 No. 30182, still coupled to its push and pull set, attaches a through coach for Waterloo to the end of an express.

An M7 locomotive arrives with a push and pull train from Yeovil Town as 'Schools' No. 30912 *Downside* backs down on to the 2.55p.m. train to Salisbury, which in the other picture, is seen leaving.

LYME REGIS BRANCH

At Axminster, No. 30582 is transferring a through coach from Waterloo to its branch train waiting in the bay platform on the 'up' side. Meanwhile No. 34072 *257 Squadron* pulls away for Exeter with the through train from Brighton to Plymouth, where it will arrive just after 6p.m.

One summer's morning No. 30582 stands outside the small one road shed at Lyme Regis, which closed in 1963.

A rare working at Lyme Regis on 20th June 1959. Nos. 30582 and 30583 join forces to handle a return holiday special to Oldham, composed of LMR stock. At Axminster, T9 No. 30719 took the train over for the run to Templecombe.

PERMANENT WAY ACTIVITY

Whilst the 'King Arthur' class were not the most suitable motive power, they could sometimes be seen on Meldon ballast trains in the early 1950s instead of the more usual S15, or N class. Here No. 30453 *King Arthur* pulls slowly out of Exeter with an eastbound working.

Very much on its home ground, for it was long a Yeovil engine, No. 31792 coasts into Yeovil Junction with a permanent way train. To the far left of the picture an LMR Class 5 waits to work an 'up' train which dates the photograph as the spring of 1953 when these engines were temporarily drafted to the Southern Region.

Gangers stand back as 'Merchant Navy' No. 35006 *Peninsular & Oriental S.N.Co.* throws up a cloud of dust from the new ballast, as it sweeps down Honiton Bank towards Seaton Junction. Long a high speed stretch of line, figures well into the 80s were common on the descent from Honiton Tunnel.

At a rather more pedestrian pace, Q1 No. 33001 comes up the main line at Raynes Park with an engineer's train, more likely as not on a Sunday morning.

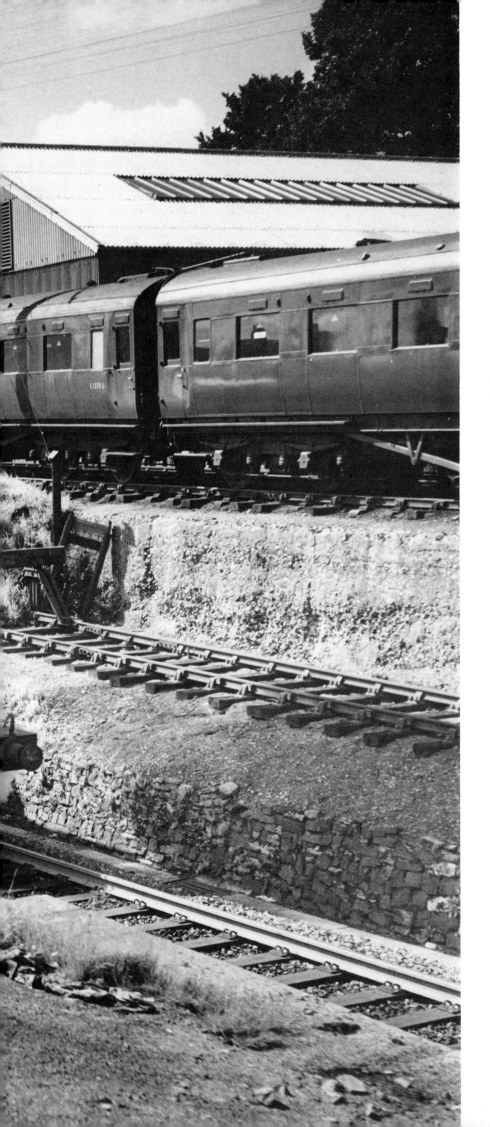

A beautifully lit picture of a ballast train from Meldon climbing the final part of the 1 in 37 gradient from Exeter St. David's to the Exeter Central, hauled by an N class 2-6-0 and M7 No. 30670.

MILK TRAFFIC

'King Arthur' No. 451 *Sir Lamorak* is approaching Malden just after the war with the afternoon milk empties from Clapham Junction to the West of England. For many years this train departed at 3.54p.m. to run via East Putney and thence to the main line at Wimbledon. In the early 1950s it was sometimes hauled by a rare (to London), Exmouth Junction 'West Country' Pacific, such as No. 34030 *Watersmeet. Below,* M7 No. 30133 is engaged in some quiet shunting of milk tank wagons over on the Windsor side at Clapham Junction.

On loan from the Western Region to Exmouth Junction Shed in 1953, Cardiff Canton's 'Britannia' No. 70028 *Royal Star* arrives at Salisbury with the 3.54p.m. milk empties from Clapham Junction. The other 'Britannias' on loan from the Western Region at this time were Nos. 70017/23/24 and 29.

The Express Dairy Depot at Seaton Junction forms the background to this picture of 'King Arthur' No. 30798 *Sir Hectimere* leaving the station with a 'down' train. This picture reflects the one-time importance of the dairy traffic on the Salisbury to Exeter line.

'CHANGE FOR SEATON'

A regular performer on the 4½ mile branch to Seaton, M7 No. 30021 stands in the 'up' main line platform by the Express Dairy Depot with a Urie push and pull set.

Down at Seaton, M7 No. 30045 is ready to leave for the junction. To the left is the engine shed opened in the late 1930s when the station was rebuilt.

The signalman takes the branch line tablet from the crew of M7 No. 30045 which has just arrived from Seaton. At the time of writing, the concrete footbridge is still in position, although all traces of the branch have vanished. To the left of the branch train, 'King Arthur' No. 30798 *Sir Hectimere* arrives with a stopping train to Exeter.

HONITON BANK

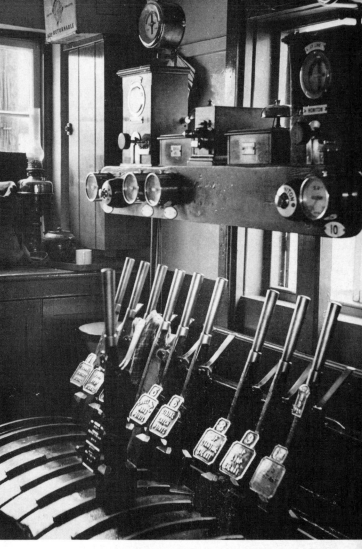

The beautifully kept interior of Honiton Incline box, lit by oil lamps after dark. The box was situated on the 'up' side of the line not far from the eastern portal of Honiton Tunnel, and its remains can still be seen. At the top of the bank, 'West Country' No. 34038 *Lynton* emerges from the 1,345yds. long tunnel on the run down to Seaton Junction.

On a damp drizzly day, 'Merchant Navy' No. 35006 *Peninsular & Oriental S.N.Co.* climbs the 1 in 80 bank past Honiton Incline box, watched by two permanent way men. Later, while a signal engineer attends to the Incline box 'down' home signal, S15 No. 30842 plods up the bank with a freight for Exeter. Today, the 'up' line has been removed and, with the growth of lineside vegetation, the scene has changed completely.

EXETER LINE FREIGHT

No. 34054 *Lord Beaverbrook* speeds past Quarry Gates box between Dinton and Tisbury with a freight. No. 34054 was never rebuilt, and in this picture still has an unmodified tender which dates the picture as pre-1963.

(*Above Right*) The monkey puzzle tree at Whimple can still be seen, but a train like this one is very much a thing of the past. Drummond 700 class No. 30327 from Salisbury, not a class much seen on the line, is in charge of an engineer's train.

(*Below Right*) Why 8P 'Merchant Navy' No. 35010 *Blue Star* is spending time shunting in Axminster Yard is unknown. The engine is in the goods shed road with the cattle dock to the left. Possibly the engine is working an 'up' freight from Exeter, and the box vans may contain Axminster carpets from the factory close to the station.

(*Below*) On the climb out of Salisbury, No. 34048 *Crediton* passes Idmiston Halt with a Templecombe to Basingstoke fitted freight.

'72A'

(*Below & Right*) Merchant Navy No. 35008 *Orient Line* is undergoing repair in the light and airy cathedral-like repair bay at Exmouth Junction Shed. The new shed was completed in 1929 and closed in 1967. These pictures give a good impression of the quite heavy repairs and examinations that main sheds were equipped to undertake.

(*Below*) In the main part of the shed, pride in the job is reflected in the attention which a member of staff is giving to the depot's splendidly kept steam breakdown crane, DS1580. Behind the crane is an old LSWR coach and a mess and tool van.

From the board on the front of the engine, Adams radial tank No. 30584 is awaiting the attention of the boilersmith after a spell of duty on the Lyme Regis branch. The side view of the same engine shows perfectly the incomparable atmosphere of the working steam shed, now alas never to be quite recaptured. No. 30584 was built by Dübs and Co. and still retains its attractive diamond-shaped works plate.

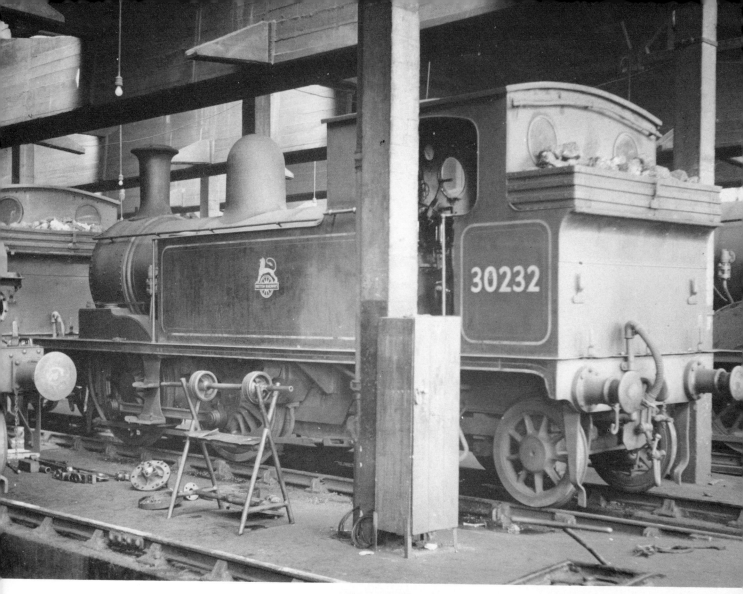

Side by side the back of the shed at Exmouth Junction, are Adams 02 No. 30232, built in 1895, and Standard Class 3 2-6-2T No. 82013, built in 1952, which is undergoing repairs to its piston valves. In the mid-1950s, Exmouth Junction's allocation was around 110 engines, only second in size on the Southern to Eastleigh.

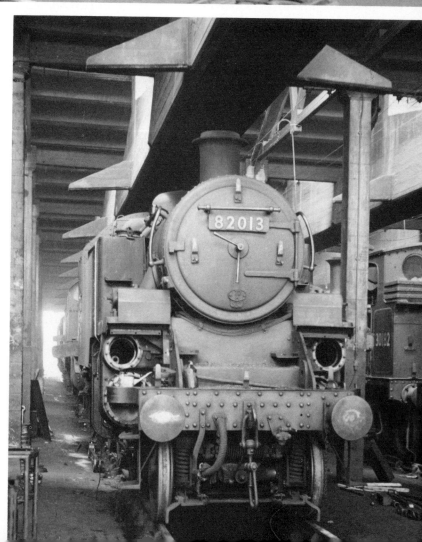

The typical scene of contrasts in motive power in the shed yard, showing two rebuilt 'Merchant Navy' Pacifics by the water tanks, together with M7s Nos. 30048 and 30670, and a T9 locomotive.

No. 34056 *Croydon* is about to enter the yard with a short freight, demonstrating the easy duties that many Exmouth Junction Pacifics were employed on. No. 34056 was among those Pacifics transferred to the Western Region at the end of 1962 due to boundary changes on the Salisbury to Exeter line, but survived almost to the end of steam on the Southern.

(*Above Right*) Z class 0-8-0 No. 30957 is out of use on the line by the south side of the shed, well placed for viewing from passing trains.

(*Below Right*) Salisbury's S15 No. 30847 is captured in between duties at Exmouth Junction. In 1960, the engine was fitted with a 6-wheeled tender from a 'King Arthur'. The engine was sold to Woodham's at Barry in 1964, but was rescued by the Maunsell Society and is being restored at the Bluebell Railway, where it is being fitted with an original pattern 8-wheeled tender.

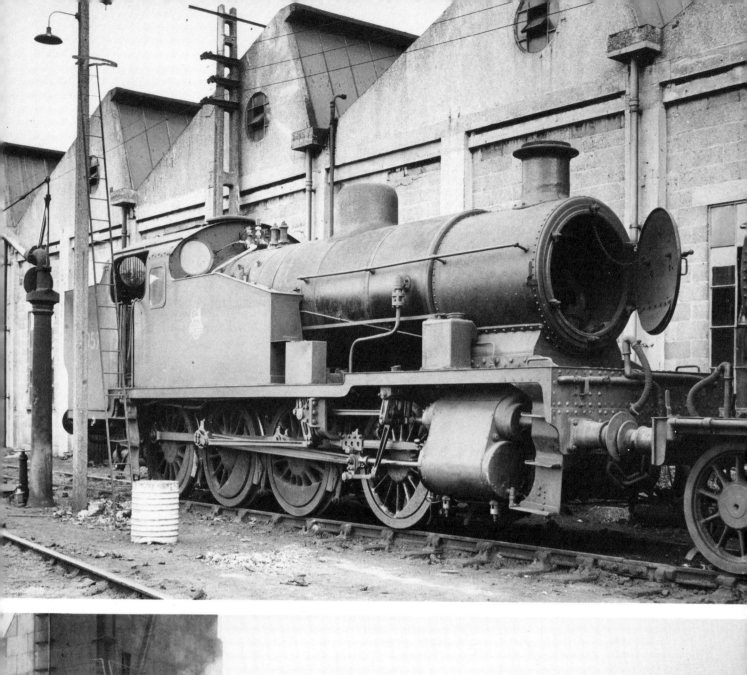

SHED DUTIES

By the water tanks at the shed, a rebuilt 'Merchant Navy' has the ash cleaned out of its smokebox, one of the dirtiest jobs of all for the shed staff.

Inside the shed a steam lance is used to clean the motion of unrebuilt Bulleid Pacific No. 34038 *Lynton*. No. 34038 finished its days on the Bournemouth line and was one of the last unrebuilt pacifics at work.

No. 30670 is attended to by a fitter. In 1959 this engine was one of the last M7s to receive a general overhaul and, judging by its condition in this picture, has not long been back from Eastleigh. No. 30670 was never push and pull fitted and would have spent its time working on the Exmouth branch or on station pilot and banking duties at Exeter Central and Exeter St. David's.

Budding footplate staff groom U class locomotive No. 31791, and tidy up some of the inevitable debris associated with any busy running shed. No. 31791 is standing on the north side of the shed, and behind the M7 on the left of the picture is the entrance to the repair shed.

At Exmouth Junction Shed, a fitter has just completed some minor adjustments to No. 35009 *Shaw Savill* before the engine works the 'up' 'Atlantic Coast Express'. Note the oil lamp over the electric light on the buffer beam ready for the light engine run to Exeter Central Station.

Off the shed and ready for action, Exmouth Junction Pacific No. 35023 *Holland Afrika Line* backs down through Black Boy Tunnel to Exeter Central to pick up the train for the journey east.

(*Right*) Comings and goings — No. 35009 *Shaw Savill*, a regular engine for the 'ACE', is captured passing Exmouth Junction signal box with the 'up' and 'down' trains. The fireman of Z class No. 30951, shunting in the yard, no doubt wishes he were on such a top link duty. The last steam-hauled 'ACE' ran in 1964. In the top picture Black Boy Tunnel can be seen in the distance, and in the foreground the Exmouth branch diverges.

Z CLASS AT WORK

The railway scene at Exeter St. David's presented a wonderful variety of trains and locomotive types in the 1950s and early 1960s. Typical of what might be seen on the Southern are these two pictures of Z class 0-8-0s Nos 30951 and 30952 piloting N class 2-6-0s, watched, in the upper picture, by the author's wife.

Another member of the class, No. 30955 banks a passenger train up the last stretch of the 1 in 37 gradient to Exeter Central. The limit for a Pacific and a Z class locomotive was ten coaches.

There is a lull at Exeter Central Station as No. 30956 waits for its next turn of duty in the 'up' relief road. For those who knew the bustle of summer Saturdays in the 1950s and 1960s, this is now a station of ghosts, disturbed only by the arrival of a Class 50 diesel on a main line train, or an Exmouth branch diesel multiple unit.

NORTH CORNWALL T9s

No. 30709 was among the last of the class to work on the North Cornwall Line from its sub-shed at Okehampton, to Halwill, Bude and Padstow. Back at its home shed of Exmouth Junction, the locomotive is out of use by the turntable road facing the main line.

En route to Padstow, No. 30717 takes water at Launceston whilst station staff load the front van, which seems to have travelled to Marks Tey, Birmingham and Waterloo recently judging by the chalked destinations on it! On Mondays to Fridays in the early 1950s, only five trains a day made this journey, including the 'ACE', which ran fast from Exeter to Halwill.

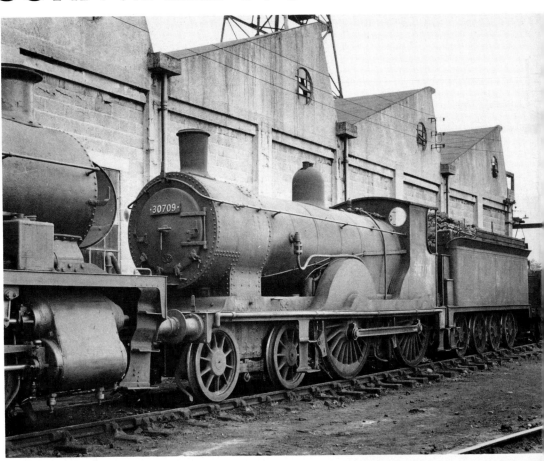

At 260 miles from Waterloo, Padstow, like nearby Wadebridge, always had a certain air of railway romance and mystique about it. The two T9s in these pictures add to this feeling No. 30710 is at the head of a train for Okehampton, and then leaving the station with No. 30717 waiting in the yard. No. 30710 was notable as being the last T9 to be superheated in 1929.

SOUTHERN RE-BORN